MW00912982

When the night is dark and lonely
And you long for love and light,
Think about the old, old story
Of a special bright star night.

This book belongs to

_____

_____

_____

Text by Lois Rock
Illustrations copyright © 1997 Louise Rawlings
This edition copyright © 1997 Lion Publishing
The author asserts the moral right
to be identified as the author of this work
Published by
Lion Publishing plc
Sandy Lane West, Oxford, England
ISBN 0 7459 3731 4
Lion Publishing
4050 Lee Vance View, Colorado Springs, CO 80918, USA
ISBN 0 7459 3731 4
First edition 1997
10 9 8 7 6 5 4 3 2 1 0
A catalogue record for this book is available
from the British Library
Printed and bound in Singapore

NIGHTLIGHTS

Bright Star Night

LOIS ROCK

ILLUSTRATED BY LOUISE RAWLINGS

A LION BOOK

The long, long wait till Christmas
Is like the long, long night
When you wake up and wait—oh, hours—
Until the morning light.

When time passes
slowly
I hope God will
come close.

When the night is
dark
I hope God will
come close.

When I long for
dull days to turn
to bright days
I hope God will
come close.

Long years ago, a people
Felt life was dark as night.
They really longed to follow God:
They never got things right.

It's so easy to copy others
Just like a sheep.

It's so easy to end up doing wrong and foolish things
Just like a sheep.

It's so easy to end up in a muddle
Just like a sheep.

But God had made a promise:
'One day, I'll send a king
who'll really help you be my friends,
who'll put right everything.'

God can help those
who are lost
**As a shepherd and a
friend.**

God can help those
who are in a mess
**As a shepherd and a
friend.**

God can help those
who are sad
**As a shepherd and a
friend.**

But who would be the mother
Of God's very special son?
God asked a girl named Mary:
She was glad to be the one.

When an angel told
Mary God's message,
she said,
'Let God's plan happen.'

Whenever God needs
good things done,
people still say,
**'Let God's plan
happen.'**

God has work for
anyone who says,
**'Let God's plan
happen.'**

Mary and the man she loved
Were far away from home
When her little boy was born
In a borrowed room.

God is richer than
anyone.
God was born a child.

God is more
important than
anyone.
God was born a child.

God is stronger than
anyone.
God was born a child.

Some shepherds on the hillsides
Were watching through the night.
An angel stood among them
And everywhere was bright.

The shepherds were
ordinary, yet an angel
brought them news:
Good news from God.

The shepherds were
poor, yet an angel
brought them news:
Good news from God.

The shepherds were
tired from working,
yet an angel brought
them news:
Good news from God.

The angel told the shepherds
About the newborn boy:
The One whom God had promised
To bring the whole world joy.

A baby was born in
Bethlehem:
Little baby Jesus.

Mary the mother,
God the father:
Little baby Jesus.

With only a manger
for his cradle:
Little baby Jesus.

The night was filled with angels
Who sang a joyful song
Praising God who'd sent his Son
To save the world from wrong.

'Glory to God in the highest,' sang the angels,
'And on earth, peace.'

'Glory to God in the highest,' sang the angels,
'And on earth, peace.'

'Glory to God in the highest,' sang the angels,
'And on earth, peace.'

Far away, some wise men
Saw a new star up above
Telling them a king was born:
Jesus, king of love.

what did the wise men bring?
Gold: a gift for a king.

what did the wise men bring?
Frankincense: a gift for someone who lives to lead people to God.

what did the wise men bring?
Myrrh: a gift for someone who dies to bring people to God... and lives again.

So you can sleep each night in peace—
Be Christmas near or far—
For Jesus' love now lights the world:

Jesus showed God's love to people.
He is the light of the world.

Jesus brought God's forgiveness to people.
He is the light of the world.

Jesus opened the way to God.
He is the light of the world.

He is its morning star.